I0845685

Resolving CloudFormation Change Set Failures

Table of Contents

Chapter 1. Introduction

In our Special Report, we delve into the realm of AWS CloudFormation and specifically focus on untangling the complex but essential topic of Resolving Change Set Failures. Although this may seem like a daunting, highly technical subject, we've anchored our approach firmly to the ground, intending to simplify and illuminate without diluting the importance or complexity of the issue. Whether you're an experienced cloud engineer or a rookie still finding your footing, this comprehensive report is engineered to navigate you through the labyrinth of potential pitfalls with CloudFormation Change Sets. Prepared to offer practical solutions, this report promises to be invaluable for anyone looking to solidify their understanding and enhance their problem-solving capabilities in this crucial aspect of cloud computing.

Chapter 2. Understanding AWS CloudFormation: An Overview

Before diving headfirst into the complex topic of resolving CloudFormation Change Set issues, it's crucial to have a solid understanding of AWS CloudFormation itself. CloudFormation is Amazon Web Service's answer to the ever-growing need of deploying cloud resources and managing them in a manner that's safe, predictable, and highly efficient.

CloudFormation presents a paradigm shift- transforming infrastructure into code. This concept follows the Infrastructure as Code (IaC) model.

2.1. The Infrastructure as Code Model

Infrastructure as Code is a practice in which infrastructure (networks, virtual machines, load balancers, and connection topology) is defined and managed using code, rather than manual processes. It evolved to solve the problems faced with infrastructure setup and maintenance, setting up a predictable mechanism to manage and provision the technology stack in an automated, efficient, and quick manner.

IaC is a key DevOps practice and is used in conjunction with continuous delivery. The benefits of an IaC approach include improved speed and reduced risk of implementing infrastructure. With IaC, DevOps teams can test applications in production-like environments early in the development cycle.

2.2. Understanding AWS CloudFormation

AWS CloudFormation provides a language (YAML or JSON) for you to describe all the AWS resources required for your application. It acts as an IaC service, supporting the practices of DevOps and agile development. It uses templates, which are simple text files, to handle and provision all the resources needed for your applications.

These CloudFormation templates describe the desired resources and their dependencies so you can launch and configure them together as a stack. You can use a template to create, update, and delete an entire stack as a single unit, as often as you need to, instead of managing resources individually. You can manage and provision stacks across multiple AWS accounts and regions.

2.3. Key Components of CloudFormation

AWS CloudFormation consists of several key components:

- **Template**: A JSON or YAML formatted text file. It describes the resources and properties.

- **Stack**: A set of related resources and properties, created, updated, or deleted as a single unit.

- **Change Set**: A summary of the proposed changes to a stack. You can view a change set before deciding whether to apply the changes to the stack.

- **StackSet**: AWS CloudFormation StackSets lets you create, update, or delete stacks across multiple accounts and regions with a single CloudFormation template.

2.4. AWS CloudFormation Workflow

Working with AWS CloudFormation involves the following steps:

1. You describe your AWS resources in a CloudFormation template.

2. CloudFormation takes that template as input and creates a stack based on your instructions.

3. You can then use AWS Management Console, SDK, or CLI to direct CloudFormation to create, update, or delete stacks.

4. As CloudFormation creates or updates a stack, you can view the resources that make up the stack and the status of the stack.

From a broader perspective, there are three main phases in the CloudFormation lifecycle: Create, Update and Delete.

- During the Create phase, a stack is born, and CloudFormation provisions specified resources based on the template.

- In the Update phase, any changes you make in the stack template result in CloudFormation updating the stack accordingly. Change sets fall in this phase.

- The Delete phase involves the deletion of the stack which automatically also deletes the resources associated with it.

2.5. AWS CloudFormation Architecture

Each AWS CloudFormation is made up of four main parts: the Template, Stack, Change Sets, and StackSets.

1. **Template**: This is a JSON- or YAML-formatted text file which provides a declaration of the AWS resources that make up a stack. The Template is the blueprint for building the stack and it can be used repeatedly to create multiple stacks.

2. **Stack**: This is simply a collection of related resources that are created, managed, and deleted as a single unit. Although a Stack can contain different types of resources (such as EC2 instances, S3 buckets, and so on), these resources are related in some way and should be managed together.

3. **Change Sets**: When you want to make changes to a stack without affecting the resources, you create a Change Set. These sets allow you to preview the changes that CloudFormation will make to your stack, without actually applying those changes.

4. **StackSets**: These are used when you want to create, update, or delete stacks across multiple accounts and regions with a single AWS CloudFormation template.

By understanding all these essential components and the baseline architecture, you'll set a solid foundation that will come in handy when navigating through the universe of managing and resolving issues with CloudFormation Change Sets.

Chapter 3. The Purpose and Essential Aspects of Change Sets

AWS CloudFormation is a fully managed service provided by Amazon Web Services that assists developers and other users in creating and providing resources. However, the service can be complex and may feel overwhelming to both advanced users and beginners. One crucial aspect within CloudFormation that demands a sound understanding is the concept of Change Sets. To aid your understanding and grasp of this service and this concept in particular, let us review the fundamentals, their importance, and key aspects.

Change sets in AWS CloudFormation are used mainly for predicting forthcoming alterations to stack resources. This is fundamentally similar to creating a blueprint before making changes to a stack. Change sets provide an overview of how diverse changes will look when implemented, without making actual modifications. If the anticipated alterations present in the change set apply, the AWS CloudFormation processes those changes.

3.1. Briefing on Stack and Change Sets

Before diving into Change Sets, let's briefly touch upon what a stack means in AWS CloudFormation. A stack is a collection of AWS resources that users can manage as a single unit. Simply put, you can create, update, and delete a collection of resources by managing stacks. You can use AWS CloudFormation to manage related resources as a single unit, rather than handling them individually.

While the purpose of a stack is the management of resources, Change Sets, on the other hand, can be considered as a simulation or 'test-run' of what changes will occur when a stack update is initiated without altering the actual stack. Change Sets list out the changes AWS CloudFormation will make, providing an opportunity to verify and validate them before actual implementation. You can spot potential mistakes and also confirm whether the changes align with your expectations.

3.2. Importance of Change Sets

Change Sets play a pivotal role in maintaining the integrity of stack modifications. A few vital reasons why Change Sets are essential in AWS CloudFormation include:

1. Avoidance of Unexpected Resource Modifications: Change Sets provide a summary of changes before actual implementation, reducing the chances of unintended resource modifications. It aids in averting the risk of failed updates and preserves the health of your stacks.

2. Detailed Overview: It can be cumbersome to visualize the effects of code or configuration alterations. Change Sets become a tool that gives a detailed overview of the expected changes, leading to more confident implementations.

3. Risk Mitigation: Change Sets can act as a checkpoint to review changes, ensuring no critical resource removals or modifications occur unintentionally.

4. Validation: It lets users review the AWS CloudFormation's interpretation of a desired state, validating the changes in terms of business and technical expectations.

Change Sets, therefore, become an important checkpoint providing users a safe environment to validate changes, thereby increasing the reliability of stack updates.

3.3. Key Aspects of Change Sets

There are several key aspects related to Change Sets that users ought to be cognizant of. Here, we delve into some of those important factors.

1. Creating and Applying Change Sets: AWS CloudFormation provides integrated commands and actions to create and apply Change Sets. In essence, users write an AWS CloudFormation template, creating a Change Set for stack modifications, and then implementing these planned changes.

2. Understanding Details of Change Sets: Each Change Set contains useful information that you need to interpret correctly to understand the implications. For example, 'Action' refers to the action AWS CloudFormation will perform, 'Replacement' denotes whether a new resource will replace an existing one, and 'ResourceType' signals various AWS resource types.

3. Identifying Safe and Unsafe Changes: AWS CloudFormation categorizes the changes into two types: 'safe to select' and 'unsafe to select'. The Change Set provides warnings for the changes that might be disruptive, guiding users on potentially risky updates.

4. Updating Stack with Change Sets: You can only update a stack with a created Change Set. After validating the Change Set, users can execute it to apply the changes described within it. Users can also delete a Change Set if they do not wish to apply the changes.

5. Estimating Cost for Change Sets: AWS CloudFormation also generates a cost estimate for your Change Sets. This allows users to understand and manage the possible financial implications before applying the changes.

The more comfortable users become with these key aspects of Change Sets, they can improve their practices around managing AWS CloudFormation stacks, bringing them more stability and resilience to their cloud resources.

AWS CloudFormation and Change Sets together streamline the process of deploying and updating various AWS resources. While stacks accelerate the process of provisioning and updating related resources together, Change Sets offer a test-run environment, enhancing the reliability of stack modifications. By understanding the purpose and critical aspects of Change Sets, users can ensure their AWS resources' efficiency, safety, and integrity.

In the following chapters, we will deepen our understanding by learning how to create and manage Change Sets and handle potential pitfalls, so stay tuned.

Chapter 4. Unpacking CloudFormation Stack and the Role of Change Sets

When dealing with AWS CloudFormation, it is instrumental to understand Stacks and Change Sets' integral roles. They form the foundation upon which CloudFormation builds and modifies resources on the AWS infrastructure. Let's begin unpacking these critical components and their involvements in managing your AWS resources.

4.1. Understanding CloudFormation Stacks

AWS CloudFormation stacks are a collection of related AWS resources that are created, modified, or deleted as a single unit. When you use AWS CloudFormation, you manage related resources in a structured, cohesive manner which allows you to visualize your resources quickly.

Consider a stack as a deployment unit, each stack is made up of resources defined by a CloudFormation template. The resources in a stack are defined by the stack's AWS CloudFormation template. You can create, update, and delete a collection of resources by creating, updating, and deleting stacks.

Moreover, all the resources in a stack are defined within the stack's AWS CloudFormation template. Once the stack is successfully created, all of its resources will be up and running as per the template definitions and configurations. If a stack creation fails, AWS CloudFormation will roll back and delete all resources created thus far. This ensures atomicity and maintains consistency in your application environment.

Stacks are also easy to manage. Built-in capabilities like tagging allow you to quickly classify and sort stacks based on your set parameters like cost center or application name.

4.2. What is a Change Set?

While stacks lay the groundwork, CloudFormation Change Sets play a crucial role in modifying these stacks. A change set, in the context of AWS CloudFormation, pertains to the summary of proposed changes to be made in a stack.

Without a change set, you won't be able to see what changes AWS CloudFormation will make to your stack. A change set includes information on what resources AWS CloudFormation will modify, create, or delete. You can then decide to implement the set to update your stack accordingly, or reject it if it's not as you intended.

This feature adds an extra layer of safety, ensuring that you are fully aware of the impact of an update before it happens. This way, you will not inadvertently disrupt your resources while trying to make modifications.

4.3. Creating and Using Change Sets

Creating a change set involves picking a stack that already exists and a template that describes the desired updates. Each change set describes the changes CloudFormation will apply to a stack. To actually apply the changes, you execute the change set.

When submitted, CloudFormation doesn't enact the changes right away; instead, it works out the differences between the current stack and the proposed one derived from the new template. It composes a detailed report listing the modifications that will take place if the change set gets enacted.

Afterwards, you can decide to either execute the change set, triggering the modifications, or abandon it if it doesn't align with your desired state. Remember, you can create multiple change sets for a single stack, but only one can be implemented at a time.

4.4. Resolving Change Set Failures

Change set failures can occur due to various reasons such as invalid template syntax, insufficient permissions, or because the specified resources do not exist. When you detect a failure, it is important to review the error message and resolve the issue that caused the failure.

For instance, if the failure occurs due to insufficient permissions, you should ensure that the AWS IAM role associated with the CloudFormation stack has enough permissions to operate on the specified resources. If the failure happens because of an invalid template syntax, you should validate the CloudFormation template using AWS Management Console, AWS CLI, or AWS SDKs before creating the change set.

Parsing CloudFormation error messages requires an understanding of AWS services and understanding why a resource operation could fail. Given the voluminous nature of AWS services and dependencies, these failures can range from logic issues in the CloudFormation template, AWS service-specific issues, or AWS CloudFormation specific issues.

To summarize, Cloud Formation stacks and Change Sets are the core mechanisms for orchestrating and evolving your AWS resources. This understanding is pivotal for efficiently managing your environment and for troubleshooting issues that can arise during the lifecycle of your resources. With this knowledge, you can confidently traverse the CloudFormation landscape and find solutions to common problems such as Change Set failures.

Inspirations drawn from this in-depth observation will hold you in good stead whether you're trying to get a handle on your costs, improve resource orchestration or enhance service stability. AWS CloudFormation is indeed a powerful tool, and its correct usage can possibly improve the resilience and operability of your AWS resource management.

Chapter 5. Common Challenges Encountered in AWS CloudFormation Change Sets

AWS CloudFormation lets you tap into a veritable sea of potential, providing the dexterity and speed needed to handle resource provisioning tasks. However, just as Icarus discovered when he flew too close to the sun, there are potential pitfalls that need to be navigated deftly to avoid a rapid nosedive into complexity and confusion.

5.1. Incorrectly Referenced Resources

One of the most common hurdles comes in the form of incorrectly referenced resources. This tends to happen when you mention a resource that hasn't been defined within your CloudFormation template.

```
Resources:
  S3Bucket:
    Type: 'AWS::S3::Bucket'
  BucketPolicy:
    Type: 'AWS::S3::BucketPolicy'
    Properties:
      PolicyDocument:
        Statement:
          - Action: 's3:*'
            Resource:
```

```
Fn::Sub: 'arn:aws:s3:::${S3BucketInvalid}'
```

In the above snippet, the bucket policy is referring to `S3BucketInvalid` which does not exist in the `Resources` section of the template. It's an easy mistake to make but one that can be remarkably frustrating.

To tackle this, double-check your template for any misspellings or references to inexistent resources. As a best practice, define your resources separately, and only after confirming their existence should you start referencing them in other resource definitions.

5.2. Stack Limit Exceeded

AWS sets certain limits on CloudFormation usage, and exceeding stack limits can lead to failures. At any given time, an AWS account can only have a maximum of 200 stacks. If you are trying to operate beyond this limit, you will encounter problems.

You can approach the issue from two angles. First, opt for stack deletion, where you remove the unneeded or obsolete stacks to make space for new ones. Alternatively, consolidate your resources into fewer, larger, and more comprehensive stacks.

5.3. Exceeding Resource-Specific Limits

Different resources within AWS have distinct limitations. For instance, an Amazon S3 bucket name must be globally unique and cannot be changed after creation. Whether it's IAM roles, EC2 instances, or Lambda functions, working within these parameters is crucial.

Keep an eye on service-specific quotas within AWS - you can check these in the AWS Service Quotas console. If you find yourself bumping against these, considering requesting limit increases to accommodate your requirements.

5.4. Invalid Template Parameters

Parameters add dynamic content to your CloudFormation templates, but these can cause problems if not handled carefully. The issues can vary from an unsupported or invalid default value to inconsistent naming.

```
Parameters:
  InstanceType:
    Type: String
    Default: t.2micro
    Description: "WebServer EC2 instance type"
```

In this case, the default value `t.2micro` is incorrect as `t2.micro` would be the correct EC2 instance type. Therefore, the template fails during the creation of the stack.

Thoroughly understanding the types and allowed values, and ensuring names are consistent throughout the template, can save you from these issues. Testing your CloudFormation stack using AWS CloudFormation Designer or creating test stacks can help validate your parameters and templates.

5.5. Circular Dependency Errors

Circular dependencies occur when two or more resources depend on each other in some way.

E.g., if you have an IAM Role that needs to be created before an EC2 instance but requires the instance's profile to be created first.

Being aware of the creation sequence of AWS resources can circumnavigate this situation. Review your template for potential circular references and split them into manageable chunks so that dependencies are resolved before they become a problem.

AWS CloudFormation offers enormous flexibility and power when it comes to orchestrating and managing resources. The challenges we have discussed above are common, but with knowledge and careful templating, they can certainly be avoided or solved. The next time you encounter a change set failure, take a step back and consider these factors.

Beyond this, AWS offers efficient debugging and validation tools such as CloudFormation Designer, StackSets, and Drift Detection which can help you troubleshoot further issues. Understanding the ins and outs of these can elevate your CloudFormation ability to the next level.

Remember, CloudFormation is complex - not because it wants to trip you up but because it wants to offer you as much flexibility and dynamic control as possible. Like a wise maestro navigating a symphony, wield the wand of CloudFormation carefully and accurately, and you will find yourself in perfect harmony with AWS cloud resources.

Chapter 6. Decoding CloudFormation Change Set Failures: A Deep Dive

AWS CloudFormation provides a structured approach for designing, deploying, and managing AWS resources. As you leverage the convenience of this Infrastructure as Code service, you may also face challenges - one being troubleshooting CloudFormation Change Set failures. Our deep dive aims to decode these issues, revealing the underlying causes and practical solutions that will streamline your work with AWS.

6.1. Understanding AWS CloudFormation

AWS CloudFormation allows you to manage AWS resources predictably and consistently via code. It outlines and provisions your AWS infrastructure, letting you automate resource deployment and configurations efficiently.

When you create a CloudFormation stack, you provide AWS with a JSON or YAML formatted template describing your desired resources and their configurations. AWS CloudFormation interprets this file and provisions the corresponding resources.

Change sets are an integral part of managing stacks in AWS CloudFormation. They allow you to preview the changes that will be made to your stack, without implementing them immediately. If a change set cannot be successfully created, you encounter a change set failure. Understanding the causes behind these failures and knowing how to resolve them is fundamental in mastering AWS CloudFormation.

6.2. Dissecting Change Sets

Before we delve into diagnosing and resolving change set failures, it's vital to understand change sets' anatomy.

Change sets summarize the changes you propose to make to your stack. They show what AWS CloudFormation will implement if you choose to execute the proposed changes. A change set contains a list of changes for every resource that is added, modified, or deleted. For each change, AWS CloudFormation provides details, such as the resource's current setting and proposed updates.

Change sets offer a risk-free way to confirm stack changes before they are implemented. This allows you to verify updates, avoiding any potential negative impact or unintended consequences on your infrastructure. Encountering change set failures can disrupt this crucial stage of resource management, hence the need to comprehend and mitigate the reasons behind such occurrences.

6.3. Common Causes of Change Set Failures

Change set failures often arise due to issues inherent to AWS CloudFormation or those related to resource specifications in stack templates. Understanding these common culprits will assist in troubleshooting.

1. Invalid template properties: Incorrect or invalid properties in your template can cause a change set failure. AWS CloudFormation validates property values against the resource specifications provided by AWS. If the template contains any invalid entries, AWS doesn't permit creation of the change set.

2. Insufficient permissions: AWS CloudFormation requires sufficient permissions to create and manage resources. If your

AWS Identity and Access Management (IAM) user lacks necessary permissions, it can lead to change set failures.

3. Changes to immutable resources: Immutable resources, such as the name of an Amazon Simple Storage Service (S3) bucket, cannot be changed once created. Trying to update these properties can result in change set failures.

4. Dependent resource modifications: If a planned change would delete a resource that other resources depend on, a failure will occur.

6.4. Diagnosing Change Set Failures

To diagnose change set failures, examine the failure message indicated in the AWS Management Console, AWS CLI, or AWS CloudFormation events. These details frequently help you understand the cause of the failure.

6.5. Resolving Change Set Failures

The resolution for a change set failure largely depends on its root cause. Here are suggestions for common problems:

1. Correcting Template Properties: Make sure to validate your templates before creating a change set. Tools like CloudFormation Linter can help identify possible mistakes.

2. Managing Permissions: Confirm your IAM user has sufficient permissions to perform all actions included in the change set. If not, adjust the user's IAM policy accordingly.

3. Managing Immutable Resources: You'll need to create a new resource with the desired attributes and then update the stack to replace the old resource with the new one.

4. Handling Dependent Resources: You can modify the stack to remove the dependencies before proceeding with the deletion.

6.6. Preventing Change Set Failures

Preventing failures, where possible, is better than resolving them. Here are good practices:

- Always validate your CloudFormation templates before creating a change set.

- Utilize Drift Detection in AWS CloudFormation to identify stack resources that have deviated from their expected configurations.

- Regularly reassess and adjust IAM policies to ensure they meet the changing requirements of your stack resources.

In conclusion, while CloudFormation change set failures can be puzzling, recognizing their causes and know-how of mitigation injects proficiency into your problem-solving arsenal. With a deep understanding of how to diagnose, rectify, and prevent these change set failures, you effectively eliminate a major stumbling block, making your AWS experience more efficient and hassle-free.

Chapter 7. Proactive Measures to Prevent Change Set Failures

It's essential to approach AWS CloudFormation with a proactive mindset to mitigate the risk of Change Set failures. While reactive measures can often solve issues once they have occurred, proactive measures help to eliminate these potential errors before they arise. This chapter will focus on proactive measures to circumvent failures in the creation and execution of AWS CloudFormation Change Sets.

7.1. Keeping Templates Simple and Modular

One of the critical axioms in software design is the KISS (Keep it Simple, Stupid) principle. The same principle applies to AWS CloudFormation templates. The argument for simplicity is potent and multi-faceted; simple templates make it easier to spot errors, enhance readability, and reduce complexity, thus improving maintainability. By breaking a monolithic template into several smaller, more manageable chunks, troubleshooting becomes considerably easier, and your codebase remains clean and navigable.

7.2. Regularly Updating Templates

Keeping the templates up-to-date with AWS service offerings is critical to prevent failures. AWS introduces new features and services regularly and deprecates old ones. Regularly updating your templates not only gives you access to the new features, but it also helps avoid failures resulting from deprecated services. AWS provides detailed documentation about their updates, and an understanding of these details can go a long way in preventing Change Set failures.

7.3. Leveraging CloudFormation Designer

When designing a CloudFormation template, it's easy to lose track of the resource dependencies or spot potential failure points. AWS CloudFormation Designer is a visual tool for creating, viewing, and modifying CloudFormation templates. By visualizing templates, you'll become more proficient at spotting issues that might not be immediately evident in a JSON or YAML file.

7.4. Testing Templates Before Deployment

Before deploying your template, it's essential that you thoroughly test it in a non-production environment to identify and rectify any potential issues. AWS offers a modeling and prototyping tool called `CloudFormation Guard` to perform rule-based testing on your templates. This helps in catching any potential pitfalls and rectifying them before the deployment stage.

7.5. Monitoring and Logging Activities

Monitoring the CloudFormation stack for any illicit actions or modifications is crucial. AWS CloudWatch and AWS CloudTrail can be utilized to monitor stack activity, log changes, and set up alarms for particular events, thus providing invaluable insights into what might cause your Change Set to fail and how to prevent it.

7.6. Using Stack Policies

Stack Policies provide a means to restrict users' stack modification abilities. Through Stack Policies, the risk of errors caused by unauthorized or inadvertently incorrect modifications is mitigated. By only allowing a specific set of actions on your stacks, you prevent unauthorized changes and protect key resources from being unintentionally updated or deleted.

7.7. Planning for Rollbacks

Rolling back actions in AWS CloudFormation can divest a faulty stack and restore it to its last known good configuration. Preparing efficiently for rollbacks involves the creation of snapshots, using interruption notices, and understanding what AWS CloudFormation does during a rollback. This can preemptively save the day and prevent any Change Set failures.

7.8. Resource Quotas

AWS services have certain resource quotas. During Change Set creation and execution, these quotas can be exceeded, causing failures. Thus, it's mandatory to understand the specific resource quotas and manage them efficiently to mitigate the risk of breaching these limits.

7.9. Security and IAM Roles

Assigning minimal, necessary permissions to IAM roles protects against unauthorized stack modifications. By attaching the principle of least privilege, you can largely eliminate the risk of malicious activities aimed at your resources.

These proactive measures represent a handful of cornerstones in your AWS CloudFormation failure prevention strategy. By digging deep into these principles and constantly evolving your approach in line with AWS's ever-growing range of services and features, you will be well-equipped to prevent Change Set failures in CloudFormation.

25

Chapter 8. Practical Guide to Troubleshooting Change Set Failures

In the practical lens of AWS CloudFormation, Change Set failures are commonplace occurrences demanding meticulous resolution tactics. This chapter is a roadmap through the labyrinth of troubleshooting these failures, providing a hands-on guide to navigate this essential terrain.

8.1. Understanding Change Sets

Change Sets in CloudFormation are a strategy to preview the changes that will be made to your stack without conducting any actions. They allow users to validate their updates before application, preventing inadvertent damage to the stack. The Change Set will list updates, if any, which would be executed on your stack. However, there are times where creating or executing Change Sets might fail, necessitating adequate troubleshooting.

8.2. Identifying the Causes of Change Set Failures

Common culprits behind Change Set failures include a surge of AWS API requests, absence of necessary permissions, an invalid template or parameter values, among other factors. Identifying the rationales helps tailor an appropriate troubleshooting approach.

```
// Code block simulating Change Set failure notification
for illustration purposes
```

```
An error occurred: ModelChangeSet - Failed to create
change set: [...]
```

Check CloudFormation's Events tab to collect valuable information about the error. Down the line, the cause might be revealed by error notifications like insufficient IAM permissions, exceeding API rate limits, or issues with your stack's template.

8.3. Managing AWS API Requests

Increase in AWS API requests can potentially trigger Change Set failures. AWS imposes a rate limit, and if you exceed it, you run into API-related errors leading to failure of your Change Set creation or execution.

For example,

```
// Code block simulating AWS ThrottlingException message

ThrottlingException: Rate exceeded
```

To handle this, use the exponential backoff algorithm to manage and space your API calls. Additionally, you can request AWS to increase your account-level rate limit.

8.4. Permissions in Play

Errors can turn up if your accounts lack the necessary permissions to create or execute the desired changes. In the IAM role, ascertain whether you have the necessary permissions to make changes to the stack and associated resources. A comprehensive IAM policy ensuring access to related services could counteract most permission-based causes.

8.5. Addressing Template Errors

Template errors could include invalid reference to resources, incompatible parameters, absence of mandatory resources, and other malformed YAML or JSON structures. The ErrorReason field in DescribeChangeSet API call can be used to identify specific template errors.

```
// Code block illustrating ErrorReason field

ErrorReason: "The submitted information didn't contain
changes..."
```

The robust CloudFormation Linter tool can be crucial in preemptively identifying and fixing template issues. It helps verify your templates against AWS resource specifications providing warnings for potential issues.

8.6. Tackling Parameter Problems

Issues with parameters might arise due to invalid or missing values when creating or executing a Change Set. Inspect to ensure that all parameters present in the template are provided with correct and valid input values.

AWS CloudFormation's ValidateTemplate API can confirm whether the input parameters' structure is valid. However, it does not guarantee the acceptance of parameter values during the actual Change Set creation or stack update.

To conclude, Change Set failures in AWS CloudFormation can range from the commonplace to the complex. This chapter aimed to serve as a comprehensive guide to understanding and troubleshooting these issues. Remember, persistence and thoroughness will serve you well through this procedure. Visualize each failure as an opportunity to refine your cloud engineering skills and deepen your understanding of AWS CloudFormation. The AWS community and support resources are always a valuable reservoir to tap into when in doubt.

Chapter 9. Case Studies: Real-world Scenarios Undertaking Change Set Failures

Running headlong into problems with CloudFormation Change Sets is a common occurrence that even seasoned engineers confront. Through several real-world case studies, we aim to simplify these problematic situations and present insightful strategies to resolve Change Set failures.

9.1. Case Study 1: Resource Does Not Support Update Operation

A particularly tricky situation arises when dealing with resources that do not support update operation. Let's consider a case of needing to update a specific parameter of an AWS::RDS::DBInstance resource.

As per AWS documentation, the `DBInstanceIdentifier` property of an AWS::RDS::DBInstance resource cannot be updated, i.e., CloudFormation does not replace the existing resource when the name changes. In such a circumstance, AWS CloudFormation would return an error, stating that the resource does not support update operation.

To resolve this issue, you would need to create a new DB Instance with a new name and then delete the old DB Instance. This can be achieved by manually creating a new AWS::RDS::DBInstance in your CloudFormation stack with a new `DBInstanceIdentifier`. After verifying the new DB instance, you can proceed to remove the old one from your stack.

This is a standard workaround strategy whenever you encounter resources that do not support update operations. The key takeaway is that you must always consult the AWS documentations of the specific resources you are dealing with to understand their properties and what they support or do not support.

9.2. Case Study 2: Insufficient IAM Permissions

In our second scenario, we encountered a situation where AWS CloudFormation was unable to execute a Change Set due to insufficient IAM permissions. In this case, CloudFormation was attempting to create an S3 Bucket resource but could not proceed because of a lack of necessary read/write permissions.

The error message you will notice would be something like the following: `API: s3:CreateBucket Access Denied`

The strategy to resolve this would be to double-check the IAM role attached to your CloudFormation stack. The IAM role needs the necessary permissions to create, read, update, and delete the resources in your CloudFormation templates.

In our case, adding the `AmazonS3FullAccess` managed policy to the IAM role did the trick. However, it is worth noting that granting full access can be considered too permissive in certain contexts. Therefore, make sure you assign the minimal necessary permissions following the best practice of the principle of least privilege (PoLP).

9.3. Case Study 3: Circular Dependency

Consider a case where the CloudFormation Stack fails to update due to a `Circular Dependency` error message. In this situation, two or more resources in the template rely on each other, either directly or indirectly.

Suppose you have an Elastic Load Balancer (ELB) dependent on an Auto Scaling Group (ASG) and the ASG is also dependent on the ELB. A cycle occurs. On updating the stack, CloudFormation needs to create a new ELB to replace the old one, but it cannot do this until the old ASG, which depends on the old ELB, is deleted.

The solution involves strategically introducing a new resource to break the dependency chain. For this, we can use an AWS AutoScaling `ReplacingUpdate` policy which ensures that all old instances of a group are terminated before new ones are launched.

To implement this, specify the `AutoScalingReplacingUpdate` policy and `WillReplace` property in your Auto Scaling group as follows:

```yaml
Resources:
  myASG:
    Type: 'AWS::AutoScaling::AutoScalingGroup'
    UpdatePolicy:
      AutoScalingReplacingUpdate:
        WillReplace: 'true'
```

Through this addition, CloudFormation will be able to delete the old ASG, update the ELB, and launch a new ASG, thus resolving the circular dependency.

These case studies demystify real-world problems encountered while dealing with AWS CloudFormation and Change Set failures and, more importantly, provide tried and tested strategies for resolving them. By understanding these scenarios and their solutions, you will save valuable time and effort and navigate the world of AWS CloudFormation with greater confidence. Remember, the key to efficiently resolving Change Sets lies in your ability to interpret failure messages and act upon them promptly, armed with sound knowledge and understanding.

Chapter 10. Leveraging AWS Tools to Mitigate Change Set Failures

In this section of the report, we'll delve deeply into the array of AWS tools that can be employed to mitigate Change Set Failures in CloudFormation. It's worth noting that the effective use of these tools often hinges upon a solid understanding of the underlying mechanisms driving Change Set generation and execution. Therefore, it's paramount to synthesize cognitive insight with technical proficiency for optimal results.

10.1. Understanding Change Set Failures

Change Set Failures, at the most basic level, stem from the discrepancies between the existing AWS resource configurations and the specifications detailed in your updated AWS CloudFormation templates. These discrepancies trigger exceptions during the process of updating stacks, consequently resulting in Change Set Failures. A strong comprehension of this process is a stepping stone in deciphering the root causes of these failures, and thus, their effective management.

10.2. AWS CloudFormation Stack Updates

Let's dedicate a brief interlude to understand how AWS CloudFormation Stack updates operate. When an update is initiated, CloudFormation generates a Change Set. This Set represents the expected changes that will be made following a successful implementation.

```
cloudformation.createChangeSet({
    StackName: "my-stack",
    TemplateBody: JSON.stringify(updatedTemplate),
});
```

This command generates a change set by comparing `updatedTemplate` with the current state of `my-stack`. Then, CloudFormation validates these changes against the existing resources.

10.3. Using AWS CloudFormation Drift Detection

CloudFormation's Drift Detection is a marked feature that is intended to aid you in this process. It allows for the proactive identification of discrepancies (termed 'drift') between stack resources and their CloudFormation templates.

Once you've initiated a drift detection operation on a stack or stack set, AWS CloudFormation checks each stack resource for drift. The results are then categorised into:

- MATCH, where the template matches the actual resource configuration.

- NOT_CHECKED, for resources you added manually or those not yet checked.

- MODIFIED, where the resource drifted from the template configuration.

```
cloudformation.detectStackDrift({
    StackName: "my-stack",
```

```
});
```

10.4. Identifying Change Set Failure Causes using AWS CLI

AWS CLI (Command Line Interface) is another essential tool to identify and analyze Change Set Failures. Specifically, the command `aws cloudformation describe-change-set` can offer rich insights into the precise causes of the failures.

```
aws cloudformation describe-change-set --change-set-name
your-changeset-name --stack-name your-stack-name
```

This command helps to elucidate detailed information about the Change Set like its status (whether CREATE_PENDING, CREATE_IN_PROGRESS, or FAILED), status reason, and the changes themselves. If the Change Set creation fails, it should provide an adequate explanation for the failure in the StatusReason field.

10.5. Mitigating Change Set Failures: a strategic approach

Creating a robust strategy to handle Change Set failures is essential. Here are a few practical steps:

- Ensure your CloudFormation templates follow best practices.

- Regularly use Drift Detection to keep resource configuration in sync with your templates.

- Use AWS CLI for detailed insights into Change Set creation and execution.

- Use AWS CloudTrail to troubleshoot Stack operations

- Continually monitor applications and resources using AWS CloudWatch.

Always remember, regularly identifying and resolving drift prevents Change Set failures, and can induce a significant improvement in the efficiency, performance, and the reliability of your AWS resources.

10.6. Summing Up

In this comprehensive look at leveraging AWS Tools for mitigating Change Set Failures, we covered the fundamentals of what triggers the generation of Change Sets, how to understand Change Set Failures, the ways AWS CLI and Drift Detection can aid in comprehending the causes of these failures, and finally - some hands-on practical suggestions for managing Change Set Failures. This understanding and proficiency in managing Change Set Failures can vastly enhance the productivity of your AWS resource management endeavors.

Chapter 11. Future-proof Strategies for CloudFormation Change Set Management

As AWS CloudFormation adoption continues to grow, it becomes increasingly essential to have robust strategies for managing your CloudFormation Change Sets. Here's how you can future-proof your Change Set Management, ensuring you're ready for anything that comes your way.

11.1. Understanding Change Sets

Before we delve further into strategies, let's first have a clear understanding of Change Sets. A Change Set in AWS CloudFormation is a summary of proposed changes that AWS will enact on a stack. It gives you the chance to examine changes without making them, allowing you to spot potential issues before you implement them.

11.2. Opt for Incremental Changes

As a rule of thumb, opting for incremental changes can help mitigate potential failures. Smaller, incremental changes are usually easier to manage and diagnose when issues arise, saving you from the dreaded "rolled back" status on your stacks.

Ensure you're familiar with both the AWS CLI and AWS Management Console, as these essential tools allow you to create, execute, and manage change sets effectively.

11.3. Control Access

Controlling who has access to your AWS environment is fundamental to your strategy. With AWS Identity and Access Management (IAM), you can create users, assign them specific permissions, and control their access to resources. IAM's fine-grained access controls mean you can specify who can create and execute Change Sets, further reducing potential risks.

11.4. Employ Versioning

AWS CloudFormation provides a simple mechanism to handle different versions of the same stack: by using different stack names. Pairing this with adequate version control systems (like Git) allows you to keep track of the changes made to your stacks over time. Including meaningful, detailed commit messages can save a lot of effort when attempting to unravel a problematic Change Set.

11.5. Automate Testing

Automation is a lifesaver when it comes to managing CloudFormation Change Sets. Automated testing tools like TaskCat enable you to test your CloudFormation templates across multiple AWS regions, capturing any potential issues before you make changes to your live stacks.

11.6. Leverage Stack Policies

Stack Policies are a potent tool in the AWS CloudFormation arsenal. They restrict actions that can be performed on a stack, protecting crucial resources from being accidentally updated, replaced, or deleted. Ensure that you understand and utilize stack policies effectively to protect your resources and minimize disruption.

11.7. Harness the Power of StackSets

CloudFormation StackSets allows you to create, update, or delete stacks across multiple accounts and regions. By controlling your Change Sets in the StackSets, you can provide consistency across your environment, minimizing the risk of differences leading to Change Set failures.

11.8. Regularly Review Changes

Finally, always review your changes thoroughly! By knowing exactly what is set to happen when a Change Set executes, you can avoid unwanted surprises. AWS's 'changes' command, which displays a summary of your pending changes, is an invaluable tool for this.

As cloud solutions evolve, Change Set Management strategies must adapt as well. By crafting a comprehensive strategy, leveraging AWS CloudFormation tools, and maintaining ongoing vigilance in your stacks, you can future-proof your CloudFormation Change Set Management and optimally navigate this ever-changing landscape. Remember, evolving is part and parcel of cloud computing. As you continue to grow and refine your skills, feel empowered knowing you're well-prepared to tackle any Change Set challenge you may encounter.

www.ingramcontent.com/pod-product-compliance
Lightning Source LLC
Chambersburg PA
CBHW071032260726
48661CB00007B/3011